Dec 21, 2004

One year and 10 days to early retirement. I have to be positive I can have the business to a solid ruby pin by then. I am having great difficulties at work. Most of it is my attitude. May God help me change it so I can retire in good health. Thats my prayer for tonight. God please change me and my bad attitude. - Peace

Jan 3, 2005

Here it is 2005 already. Lets list the dreams I have for this year

1) Retire so I can be at the kids functions
2) Share the business with many new friends to share with them the way to financial freedom and giving back to God.
3) Get out of debt
4) Set up an account for the girls Nolyn + Nicole
5) Give Gil + Donna a new leg (ruby)
6) loose 20 - 25# by year end.

Thank you God for guiding me in achieving these dreams.